To Appa & Amma, for everything;
to Krishnan, for his unwavering support;
to Mira & Mihir, for leading me to my passion.
To Kailash-ji, whose courage and vision
give hope and inspiration.

To all readers—*awaken the hummingbird inside you!*
—SV

To my husband Carl, for being my confidante,
constant support and endless source of inspiration.
To Saoirse, my cherished little light, may you always
remember you can achieve all your heart desires,
little by little, drop by drop.
—DSP

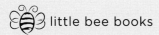 little bee books

Text copyright © 2024 by Srividhya Venkat
Illustration copyright © 2024 by Danica da Silva Pereira
Manufactured in China   RRD 0424
First Edition
10 9 8 7 6 5 4 3 2 1
Library of Congress Cataloging-in-Publication Data
is available upon request.
ISBN 978-1-4998-1569-6 (hardcover)
ISBN 978-1-4998-1570-2 (ebook)

littlebeebooks.com

For information about special discounts on bulk purchases,
please contact Little Bee Books at sales@littlebeebooks.com.

Seeker of Truth

Kailash Satyarthi's Fight to End Child Labor

written by
Srividhya Venkat

illustrated by
Danica da Silva Pereira

When Kailash Sharma was a little boy,
he heard the story of how a hummingbird
tried to put out a forest fire.
While all the other animals fled,
the tiny bird brought water in its beak
to douse the fierce flames.

Every day on his way to school, five-year-old Kailash saw another boy his age shining shoes with his father, a cobbler.

Why isn't the boy going to school? Kailash wondered.

One day, he asked the cobbler.

The man replied,
"My father was a cobbler,
I am a cobbler, and so,
my son will be
a cobbler too."

Kailash was puzzled.
*Why can't the boy choose
what he wants to be?*

Over the next few years,
Kailash began to notice things
he hadn't noticed before.
Children, like the cobbler's son,
were not allowed to do things
that Kailash could do
or go to places he could.

*Why are their lives so
different from my own?*

Like the hummingbird in the story,
Kailash wanted to help.
But he was just a kid.

What can I do?

At ten years old, Kailash decided to form a soccer club
and run snack stalls to raise money
so children who could not afford school
would be able to attend.

He also started a book bank,
collecting used textbooks from those
who no longer needed them, to lend
to those who couldn't afford them.

By the time he was a teenager,
Kailash had helped many children.

Little by little.

Drop by drop.

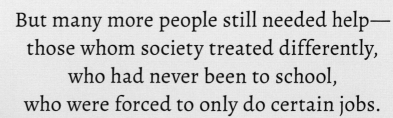

But many more people still needed help—
those whom society treated differently,
who had never been to school,
who were forced to only do certain jobs.

Jobs like sweeping streets or
cleaning toilets and sewers.
Jobs that some considered
filthy and shameful.

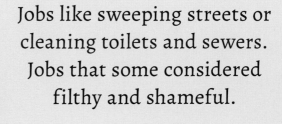

The people who did these jobs were shunned by a society that labeled them

"untouchable."

Why aren't all people given respect?
Kailash thought.

When he heard leaders promise
to end this unfair practice,
Kailash was hopeful.
He invited them to eat a meal
cooked by "untouchables."

But none of the leaders showed up! Kailash's hopes of change were crushed.

He took a stand and ate the lovingly cooked meal.

It was something no one had done before!

His parents were angry with him.
His community was angrier.
But Kailash was angriest of all.
He wanted to change the world.
But he was just one person.

*How can I alone
make a difference?*

After graduating from college, Kailash became a teacher.

But he was restless.

He wanted to do more.

To be more.

To change the world.

Kailash quit his job and changed his last name
to Satyarthi, which means "seeker of truth."
He wanted everyone to know how tough life was
for those in need.

So he started a magazine to share their stories.

His writings reached
a man named Wasal Khan,
who came to him for help.

Wasal asked Kailash to write
about his daughter, who was being
forced to work at a brick factory.

But Kailash wanted to do more.

*What if this girl was my
daughter or sister?*

Kailash could no longer wait
to make change happen.

Little by little.

Drop by drop.

It was time.

Kailash rushed to the brick factory,
where he found Wasal's daughter
and many other children too.
He tried to save them all,
but the factory owner's men stopped him.

Kailash refused to accept that
the shackles of slavery could be
stronger than the quest for freedom.
So he fought for the release of the children
until they were freed
and reunited with their families.

In the following weeks,
other people knocked on
Kailash's door,
and he rescued many more children
who were being forced to work.

Children who made toys,
but never played with them.

Children who worked in factories
and hadn't seen sunlight in years.

Children who worked in mines,
quarries, and other unsafe places.
They were children who were
not free to be children.

When Kailash rescued them,
he saw light in their eyes.
It guided him,
illuminating his path
to change the world.

Little by little.

Drop by drop.

Kailash was no longer alone.
The drops of water had multiplied.
He now had people by his side.

Together, they worked
to save more children from forced labor,
to reunite them with their families,
to help them go to school.

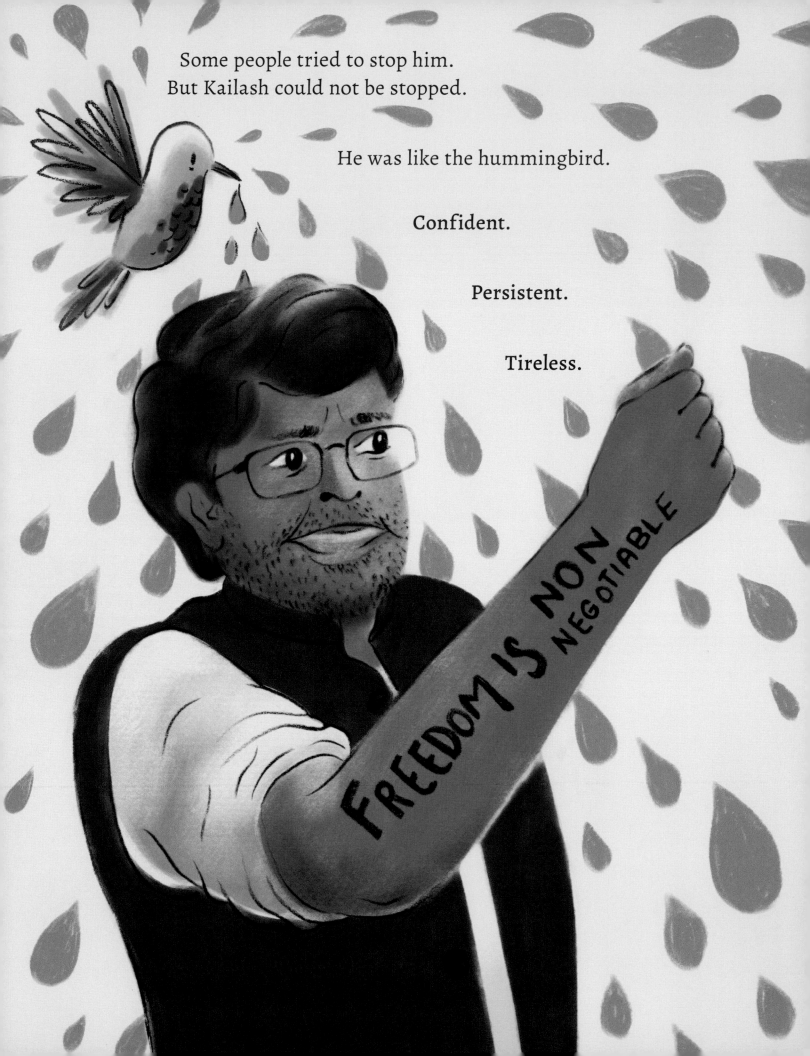

Some people tried to stop him.
But Kailash could not be stopped.

He was like the hummingbird.

Confident.

Persistent.

Tireless.

Kailash fought for new child labor laws and set up centers for
rescued children—safe, loving homes for their health and healing,

where they would learn, prepare for the future,
and help bring prosperity to their villages.

Kailash traveled to other countries and met world leaders, demanding plans to end child labor and to make education a part of every child's life.

With inspiration from leaders like Mahatma Gandhi, Nelson Mandela, and Martin Luther King, Jr., Kailash organized several marches, including the Global March Against Child Labor.

More than 7 million people paraded across 103 countries. It led to the signing of an agreement by many countries of the world, united in their stand against child labor.

When Kailash's life's work was recognized,
he reminded the world about the power of working together.
"I call for a march from exploitation to education,
I call for a march from poverty to shared prosperity,
a march from slavery to liberty,
and a march from violence to peace."

As a child, Kailash had a vision
of the cobbler's son sitting beside him at school.
As an adult, he has a vision of a world where
every child has the right to their childhood.

"My only aim in life is that every child is free
to be a child, free to grow and develop,
free to eat, sleep, and see daylight,
free to laugh and cry, free to play and learn,
free to go to school, and above all,

free to dream."

AUTHOR'S NOTE

Kailash Satyarthi was awarded the Nobel Peace Prize in 2014 (as co-recipient with Malala Yousafzai) for his selfless efforts to save children from exploitation and help them get their right to an education. He has worked tirelessly for over 40 years to free more than 100,000 children from slavery.

Since he was a child, Kailash was curious about his world—observing, asking questions, and forming opinions about right and wrong. He even questioned social norms and raised his voice for the rights of others.

When he grew up, he quit his well-paying job and started a magazine called *Sangharsh Jaari Rahega* (*The Struggle Shall Continue*) to raise awareness about the struggles of the underprivileged. Through his writings, he wanted to eliminate bias and change unfair norms, including the hiring of children as cheap labor in businesses and households.

In 1980, Kailash founded the Bachpan Bachao Andolan (BBA), or Save Childhood Movement, with the help of friends, volunteers, and supporters. Members of BBA risked their lives to conduct raid and rescue operations to save children who were being forced to work in factories, mines, quarries, the circus, and many other places. Kailash set up rehabilitation centers called Mukti Ashram, or Freedom Shelter, to help rescued children recover from their distressing experiences, and later on, get back on their feet to gain an education at the Bal Ashram or Child Shelter. He also created hundreds of "child-friendly" villages called Bal Mitra Gram (BMG) where children had a voice in bringing positive changes to their communities.

India lacked effective child labor laws at the time. Kailash persistently fought for them. His efforts led to the passing of the Child Labour (Prohibition & Regulation) Act in 1986. Today, children in India under fourteen years of age are not allowed to work (except to help family businesses before or after school hours).

Observing the excessive use of child labor in the carpet weaving industry, Kailash launched a social labeling system called Goodweave (formerly Rugmark), which labeled and certified carpets that were made without child labor. This initiative increased consumer awareness and decreased the demand for non-certified carpets. Eventually, there was a significant decline in the employment of children in the carpet industry.

Recognizing that child labor was a global problem, Kailash advocated international laws against child slavery. He organized several protest marches, including the historic Global March Against Child Labor in 1998 which involved more than 7 million people across 103 countries. It led to the passing of a key international agreement that was signed by all 187 member countries of the International Labour Organization (ILO).

Kailash also co-founded the Global Campaign for Education in 1999, a movement to promote education as a basic human right so every child could go to school. Through his theory of the "triangular paradigm," he established that education was crucial to battling child labor and poverty.

Today, Kailash continues to fight injustice. Many of the rescued children have grown up to become teachers, doctors, lawyers, social workers, and supporters who are carrying on his work and paying it forward.

CHILD LABOR TODAY

Unfortunately, child labor continues to exist today. It is estimated that 160 million children around the world were working in 2020. Of them, 56 percent were in the 5–11 age group.

The pandemic reversed much of the progress made in the past two decades in reducing child labor. Food shortage, unemployed parents, and school closures were some factors that led to a rise in child employment. However, nonprofit organizations such as Kailash's BBA continue to pursue their mission relentlessly.

The International Labor Organization (ILO) declared June 12 as World Day Against Child Labor to bring attention to the global problem and promote efforts to eliminate it.

A NOTE ON THE CASTE SYSTEM

The caste system divides society into four main groups. The first three groups—the Brahmins (priests and teachers), the Kshatriyas (kings and warriors), and the Vaishyas (merchants and farmers)—are the "upper" castes. The fourth group, Shudras (laborers), is the "lower" caste. People perform the occupation allocated to their caste throughout their lives. Outside the realm of the caste system are the Dalits, positioned as lower than the "lower" caste and left to perform undesirable "menial" work, such as cleaning streets, sewage, and toilets. They are labeled "untouchables" due to the belief that not only their mere touch, but even their shadow, can taint others. The Dalits are prohibited from mingling with others and not allowed to attend schools or visit public places. A few years after his meal with the so-called "untouchables," Kailash renounced his last name, Sharma, which indicated his "upper" caste connection. Instead, he adopted a new last name which defined his mission: Satyarthi, the seeker of truth. Although Indian constitution laws forbid caste inequalities, and the growth of cities has given more flexibility in occupation choices and intermixing, segregation and caste discrimination continue to exist even today.

SELECTED BIBLIOGRAPHY

Child Labour Free Mica. "Child Friendly Village Model." YouTube video. Uploaded on May 18, 2021. https://www.youtube.com/watch?v=duCXXOKH3Fw.

Kailash Satyarthi Children's Foundation. "Get Involved." Accessed October 18, 2023. https://satyarthi-us.org/get-involved/.

Kailash Satyarthi Children's Foundation India. "Watch How an Incident in Nobel Peace Laureate Kailash Satyarthi's Childhood Impacted & Inspired Him." YouTube video. Uploaded on November 14, 2021. https://www.youtube.com/watch?v=GT4euco-CzI.

Nobel Peace Prize Concert. "Kailash Satyarthi 2014 Nobel Peace Prize Concert Speech." YouTube video. Uploaded on October 12, 2015. https://www.youtube.com/watch?v=9AJfv5pgxZE.

Official – Global March Against Child Labour. "Kailash Satyarthi: A Journey." YouTube video. Uploaded on October 28, 2015. https://www.youtube.com/watch?v=6zn7IR6WkiI.

Pallardy, Richard. "Kailash Satyarthi." In *Encyclopaedia Britannica Online*. Last modified October 8, 2023. https://www.britannica.com/biography/Kailash-Satyarthi.

FURTHER READING

RESCUED CHILDREN MAKING A DIFFERENCE

The KidsRights Foundation. "2006 - Om Prakash Gurjar (14), India." Last accessed October 19, 2023. https://www.kidsrights.org/advocacy/winners/om-prakash-gurjar/.

Rahman, Azera Parveen. "The HINDU: Child Labourers to Champions." Kailash Satyarthi Children's Foundation. Last modified Februrary 1, 2023. https://satyarthi-us.org/the-hindu-child-labourers-to-champions/.

Srivastava, Rohit and Singh Kanishk. "These 4 Children Escaped Child Labour to Become Changemakers with Help of Kailash Satyarthi's Foundation." SocialStory. Last modified January 11, 2022. https://yourstory.com/socialstory/2022/01/child-labour-kailash-satyarthi-children-foundation?utm_pageloadtype=scroll.

World's Children's Prize Foundation. "Amar Lal, India." Last accessed October 19, 2023. https://worldschildrensprize.org/amarlal.

OTHER CHILDREN'S BOOKS ON CHILD LABOR

Hinrichs, Alexandra S. D., and Michael Garland. *The Traveling Camera: Lewis Hine and the Fight to End Child Labor.* Los Angeles: Getty Publications, 2021.

Katz, Rosie. *The Story of How I Met Kailash Satyarthi.* Scotts Valley, CA: CreateSpace Independent Publishing Platform, 2017.

Saller, Carol. *Working Children.* Minneapolis: Carolrhoda Books, 1998.

Winter, Jonah, and Nancy Carpenter. *Mother Jones and Her Army of Mill Children.* Toronto, ON: Schwartz & Wade Books, 2020.